HAWAII

GALLERY BOOKS
An Imprint of W. H. Smith Publishers Inc.
112 Madison Avenue
New York City 10016

This edition first published in U.S.
in 1990 by Gallery Books,
an imprint of W.H. Smith Publishers, Inc.
112 Madison Avenue, New York, New York 10016

ISBN 0-8317-8836-4

Printed and bound in Spain

For rights information about the photographs in
this book please contact:

The Image Bank
111 Fifth Avenue, New York, N.Y. 10003

Producer: Solomon M. Skolnick
Author: Pamela Thomas
Design Concept: Leslie Ehlers
Designer: Ann-Louise Lipman
Editor: Madelyn Larsen
Production: Valerie Zars
Photo Researcher: Edward Douglas
Assistant Photo Researcher: Robert Hale

Title page: Double-hulled canoes such as this were used by the Polynesians who traveled from the South Pacific to Hawaii in the 6th century A.D. Opposite: For decades, Aloha Tower has been welcoming visitors who arrive in Honolulu by ship. From its observatory can be seen magnificent views of the city.

Opposite: *High-rises, ancient mountains, and sailboats in the harbor—all emblems of Honolulu.* This page: *The city of Honolulu, seen from a rise.* Below: *The purpose of outrigger, seen on the port side of these canoes, is to provide stability in rough waters.*

Women adorned with fragrant flowers, undulating the mysterious hula. Thirty-foot waves crashing onto remote beaches. Fiery volcanoes smoking against an azure sky. Quiet grottoes bursting with exotic flowers and birds. Luaus pungent with the aroma of roasting pig. These are but a few of the sensual images Hawaii evokes.

Located 2,400 miles west of the U.S. Mainland, the fiftieth state is made up of a 1,600 mile-long chain of 132 islands in the middle of the Pacific Ocean. Only eight of the 132 islands are developed, and only seven of those are inhabited. Nevertheless, these tiny islands combine to create not only America's most fascinating state, but also one of the world's most dazzling sites.

In many ways, the entire development of Hawaii has much to do with geology. Between 25 and 40 million years ago, during the course of 1,000 years, huge volcanoes bubbled up from the floor of

This page: *Waikiki Beach, once the favored swimming spot of the Hawaiian* alii *(nobility). A kaleidoscope of color and form—a typical Hawaiian sunset.* Opposite: *One of scores of big hotels and apartment houses that line Waikiki Beach. Its façade, a mosaic of the radiant colors one associates with Hawaii.*

Preceding page: *Honolulu at sunset, an exquisite meld of man-made and natural beauty.* This page: *The statue of King Kamehameha I, which stands in front of Aüolani Hale (the judiciary building in downtown Honolulu) is draped with leis on Kamehameha Day, June 11, the holiday that commemorates the unification of the Hawaiian Islands.* Right: *The coat of arms outside the Iolani Palace is a reminder of Hawaii's royal past.* Opposite: *Iolani Palace, completed in 1882 by King David Kalakaua, proudly proclaims itself "the only royal palace on American soil."*

DEDICATED
TO THE ETERNAL MEMORY
OF OUR GALLANT SHIPMATES
IN THE USS ARIZONA
WHO GAVE THEIR LIVES IN ACTION
7 DECEMBER 1941

FROM TODAY ON THE USS ARIZONA
WILL AGAIN FLY OUR COUNTRY'S FLAG
JUST AS PROUDLY AS SHE DID ON THE
MORNING OF 7 DECEMBER 1941
I AM SURE THE ARIZONA'S CREW WILL
KNOW AND APPRECIATE WHAT WE ARE
DOING   A. W. RADFORD USN
7 MARCH 1950

MAY GOD MAKE HIS FACE
TO SHINE UPON THEM
AND GRANT THEM PEACE

the Pacific. Kure atoll, at the northwestern end of the chain and now a mere reef, is the oldest of the islands while the Big Island of Hawaii, with its active volcanoes, is the youngest. Many theories have been advanced to explain the emergence of the chain, but the most current avows that the archipelago was squeezed up by a single "hot spot" that spewed lava, creating islands in a sort of assembly-line fashion. Today, the "hot spot" resides under the island of Hawaii, accounting for the only still-active volcanoes in Hawaii. As the islands move westward over the next millennia, a new island may be born.

This page and opposite: *Arizona Memorial at Pearl Harbor honors those who died during the attack on the naval base on December 7, 1941. Built directly over the* Arizona, *the 184-foot long memorial slopes toward the middle, as if crushed, yet rises at either end, thus signifying ultimate victory. The staff of the flag is embedded in the scarred hull of the* Arizona.

THE SOLEMN PRIDE
THAT MUST BE YOURS
★★ TO HAVE LAID ★★
SO COSTLY A SACRIFICE
UPON THE ALTAR
OF FREEDOM

Given its remote location, Hawaii was not inhabited until the Polynesians arrived in the sixth century A.D., after having traveled across thousands of miles of ocean. Sailing in elaborate double-hulled canoes that could carry as many as 50 people, the Polynesians brought roots, seeds, dogs, chickens and pigs, and first settled on the island of Kauai. The second wave of Polynesians, probably from Tahiti, arrived about 1200 A.D., and from this moment on, the Polynesians voyaged back and forth from their homeland frequently—no doubt to fetch relatives, animals and seeds.

Although ships from Europe or the Orient may have stopped there earlier, the first confirmed landing by a European was not recorded until January 18, 1778, when British explorer Captain James Cook discovered the Hawaiian Islands while sailing north from Tahiti to reach the North American continent. Like the first

This page: *In the Punchbowl Crater are the graves of the more than 25,000 servicemen and women who died in battle during World War II, Korea and Vietnam. Pictured here, the Court of the Missing at the National Cemetery of the Pacific. Opposite: This representation of Father Damien, the priest who worked with the lepers at Molokai, is outside the new State Capitol, completed in 1969.*

Hawaiian music and dance are performed by many generations of islanders, some of whom, like this woman, are native Hawaiians. Below: *The hula, once banned by the missionaries, is now the focus of week-long festivals.*

Polynesians, he landed initially at Kauai. Cook spent two weeks exploring the islands and trading with the islanders who thought him to be Lono, god of agriculture and fertility. Upon his departure, Cook named the area the Sandwich Islands, in honor of the First Lord of the admiralty, the Earl of Sandwich.

In November 1778, Cook returned to Hawaii, "the Big Island," and again was greeted with warmth and respect. Within weeks, however, the islanders changed their minds about him and decided that he was not a god but a mere mortal. During a skirmish over a stolen cutter in 1779, Captain Cook—and 17 Hawaiians—were killed.

At the time of Cook's visits, each of the islands was ruled by a local chief. By 1795, the main islands, with the exception of Kauai and Niihau, were united (in some cases after bloody battle) under King Kamehameha I, and by 1810, all the islands came under his rule. Although King Kamehameha's tactics were not always to everyone's liking, he is revered as the great unifier of the Hawaiian Islands. The Kamehameha kings always considered themselves to be worldly, and in 1819, Kamehameha II abolished human sacrifice, which had been permitted by the Hawaiian religion.

Within twelve months of the king's decree, a group of Protestant missionaries came from Boston and settled in Hawaii. In a short time, they converted many of the islanders to Christianity. The impact of the missionaries on Hawaiian society was profound: they had "clothed the naked," produced a written Hawaiian language, taught reading and writing to the islanders, and introduced wooden churches and houses like those in New England. They also banned the hula.

Initially, the major sources of income for the islands came from farming and the exportation of sandalwood to China. By the 1830s, the sugar cane industry was underway, and it flourished during the Civil War when the South cut off the importation of sugar cane to ports in the North. Although not indigenous to the islands, pineapples were imported as early as 1813, and commercial production grew rapidly in the late nineteenth century after plants were brought in from Jamaica. Both the sugar cane and the pineapple industries were developed by American entrepreneurs, a fact that would prove pivotal to Hawaiian history.

Islanders joyfully celebrate Kamehameha Day on June 11 with festivals and parades and by dancing the hula, which King David Kalakaua believed to be "the language of the heart and therefore the heartbeat of the Hawaiian people." Below: Boldly printed patterns such as these will find their way into muumuus and aloha shirts.

Opposite: *Gathering coconuts for a festive luau in Paradise Cove, noted for its exotic birds and lush gardens.* This page: *Here a young man demonstrates the Polynesian method of gathering coconuts.* Below: *Washington Place, the Governor's Mansion, reflects New England's influence on "old" Honolulu.*

The growth of agricultural production coupled with the depletion of the local labor force—due primarily to diseases introduced by foreign sailors and others *haoles*, or white men—led to the importation of laborers from other countries and the onset of Hawaii's multinational population. First came the Chinese, followed by the new Polynesians, the Japanese, Filipinos, Koreans, and later, the Portuguese and Puerto Ricans. Ultimately more than ten different nationalities combined to form a fascinating mélange.

At Sea Life Park on Makapuua Point on eastern Oahu, dolphins perform a water ballet at the Science Theater, while nearby the Hawaiian Reef Tank, a 300,000-gallon re-creation of an undersea Pacific reef, supports a host of rare marine species.

"Chinaman's Hat," a popular landmark off the east coast of Oahu. Below: The windward, or east side of Oahu.

By the end of the last century, the balance of power between the Hawaiian monarchy and the rich, white landowners and developers began to shift. Leery of the monarchy and desiring to ensure a strong market for their products, the landowners and industrial magnates overthrew the last Hawaiian monarch, Queen Liliuokalani, in 1893. The revolutionaries created the Republic of Hawaii and made Judge Sanford B. Dole, the pineapple king, the first and only president.

But almost immediately, American planters and businessmen realized they needed even greater protection as well as certain tax advantages, and so they set out to persuade the United States to annex Hawaii. The businessmen proved a powerful lobby. In August 1898, the Hawaiian Islands became a U.S. territory and Judge Dole was appointed governor.

Opposite: *The Koolau Range runs down the center of Oahu and offers many such formidable views. This page: The mountains that surround the Valley of the Temples are among the most spectacular in the islands. A replica of Japan's Byodo-In Temple was built in the Valley of the Temples on Oahu, to commemorate the centennial of Japanese immigration to Hawaii.*

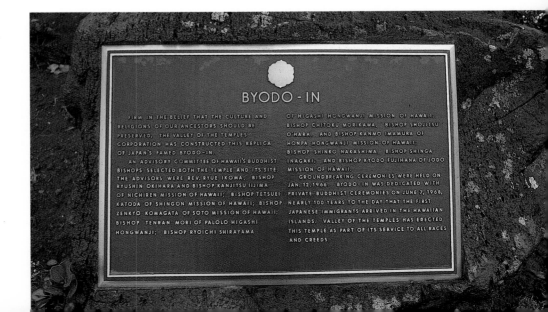

BYODO - IN

FIRM IN THE BELIEF THAT THE CULTURE AND RELIGIONS OF OUR ANCESTORS SHOULD BE PRESERVED, THE VALLEY OF THE TEMPLES CORPORATION HAS CONSTRUCTED THIS REPLICA OF JAPAN'S FAMED BYODO-IN.
AN ADVISORY COMMITTEE OF HAWAII'S BUDDHIST BISHOPS SELECTED BOTH THE TEMPLE AND ITS SITE. THE ADVISORS WERE REV. RYUE IKOMA, BISHOP RYUSHIN OKIHARA AND BISHOP KANJITSU IIJIMA OF NICHIREN MISSION OF HAWAII; BISHOP TETSUEI KATODA OF SHINGON MISSION OF HAWAII; BISHOP ZENKYO KOMAGATA OF SOTO MISSION OF HAWAII; BISHOP TENRAN MORI OF PALOLO HIGASHI HONGWANJI; BISHOP RYOICHI SHIRAYAMA

OF HIGASHI HONGWANJI MISSION OF HAWAII; BISHOP CHITOKU MORIKAWA, BISHOP SHOJITSU O'HARA, AND BISHOP KANMO IMAMURA OF HONPA HONGWANJI MISSION OF HAWAII; BISHOP SHINKO NAKASHIMA, BISHOP SHINGA INAGAKI, AND BISHOP KYODO FUJIHANA OF JODO MISSION OF HAWAII.
GROUNDBREAKING CEREMONIES WERE HELD ON JAN. 12, 1966. BYODO-IN WAS DEDICATED WITH PRIVATE BUDDHIST CEREMONIES ON JUNE 7, 1968, NEARLY 100 YEARS TO THE DAY THAT THE FIRST JAPANESE IMMIGRANTS ARRIVED IN THE HAWAIIAN ISLANDS. VALLEY OF THE TEMPLES HAS ERECTED THIS TEMPLE AS PART OF ITS SERVICE TO ALL RACES AND CREEDS.

Preceding page: *The Byodo-In Temple is set in a garden filled with tropical plants and populated with peacocks and swans.* Opposite: *One of the treasures of Byodo-In Temple.* This page: *The "Pageant of Long Canoes," a Samoan ceremony, is the highlight of a visit to the Polynesian Cultural Center, which features replicas of seven South Seas villages. Haiku Gardens, near Kaneohe, a paradise of ponds and groves.*

Preceding page: *Pupukea Beach on Oahu's north shore*. This page: *Surfers and a tranquil sea*.

Top to bottom: *Surfers riding the biggest and best-shaped waves in the world. Strictly for experts, Sunset Beach, Waimea Bay and the Banzai Pipeline on Oahu's north shore offer thrilling surfing experiences. Once Hawaiian royalty surfed to prove the worthiness of their leadership, and even Captain Cook commented on the "supreme pleasure of the surfer."*

Recognizing the strategic value of the islands, the United States Navy began construction of a large base at Pearl Harbor, which decades later would be bombed and bring the United States into World War II.

Those responsible for creating the Hawaiian Republic, and who later lobbied for annexation, began pushing as early as 1903 for Hawaiian statehood. President Harry Truman recommended that Hawaii be admitted to the Union, but it took until August 21, 1959 before Hawaii became the fiftieth state.

Today the descendants of the plantation laborers, *haoles*, and native Hawaiians live harmoniously in this tropical paradise. Hawaii's residents have borrowed freely from each other's heritage and the result is an appealing local culture. What's more, each of the eight major islands bears a personality all its own, and like its residents, unite to create a fascinating entity.

OAHU

Although Oahu is only the third-largest of the islands, it is the most populated (over 800,000 people) and boasts Hawaii's most important city and state capital, Honolulu. Also located on Oahu are several sights synonymous with Hawaii: Pearl Harbor; Diamond Head, Hawaii's "Rock of Gibraltar"; and Waikiki Beach, arguably the most famous beach in the world. Oahu is also the location of such remarkable sights as the Sea Life Park; the Polynesian Cultural Center; the Punchbowl, a crater that is the final resting place of members of the Armed Forces who died in World War II, Korea and Vietnam; and Iolani Palace, where the Hawaiian royal family lived.

Oahu is made up of two parallel mountain ranges— the Koolau and the Waianae— separated down the middle by a fertile valley. Honolulu and its suburbs occupy most of the southwestern part of the island, while the east coast is made up of calm, luxurious beaches set against the fluted cliffs of the Koolau Range. The north shore prides itself on its famed "surfers beaches," particularly Sunset Point and the Banzai Pipeline.

This page and opposite: *Akaka State Park, a 66-acre forest preserve on Hilo, boasts many dazzling waterfalls, including Akaka Falls* (opposite) *and Hapuna Falls* (below). *In Hawaiian legend, the god Akaka fell to his death from Kahuna Falls, and two other falls, Lehua and Maile, were named for his mistresses who were unable to control their tears after his death. Kahili ginger plants grow in profusion.*

This page: *Puuhonua O Honaunau National Historical Park (the City of Refuge) in the Kona district of Hawaii was once a haven for defeated warriors or those who had broken a* kapu, *or taboo. These wooden figures, called* tikis, *are hand-carved replicas of the original refuge gods. Opposite: The Painted Church at Sikona, a folk-art masterpiece. Around 1900 a Belgian priest painted exquisite* trompe l'oeil *murals that embody Hawaiian and Christian motifs.*

Opposite: *St. Peter's Church at Kahaluu on the Kona coast, also known as "the Little Blue Church," is the antithesis of its namesake in Rome.* This page: *Honomu, a farm town on the Hamakua coast, is famous for its clapboard general store which sells ice-cold sugar cane, fresh macadamia nuts, and turn-of-the-century pictures of the area.* Below: *A 27-foot monument to Captain James Cook stands on the west coast of Hawaii's near where he was killed in 1779.*

HAWAII

"The Big Island" covers an area of over 4,035 square miles, almost twice the land mass of all the other Hawaiian islands combined. The island is best known for its two remarkable mountain peaks, Mauna Kea and Mauna Loa, which rise more than 13,000 feet above sea level, and surprisingly have enough snow to support reasonably good skiing conditions. Mauna Loa, the focal point of Hawaii Volcanoes National Park, is one of the most active volcanoes in the world. Although certain parts of this region have been badly "burned" by flowing lava, much of the island offers a delightfully varied climate and terrain resulting in abundant rain forests, rich grasslands and sublime beaches.

The largest town, Hilo, sprawls around Hilo Bay, and modern resort areas dot the coast north of the city. North Kohala, the boyhood home of Kamehameha I, remains an exotic, virtually untouched region, and the City of Refuge National Historic Park on the west coast offers a mesmerizing glimpse of ancient Hawaiian culture.

The verdant Hamakua coast on the northeast edge of the Big Island is slashed with steep waterfalls that tumble into the sea. Below: Black Sand Beach, on the Puma coast of the Island of Hawaii, was formed when lava hit the sea, exploded into bits, and then was ground fine by the crashing surf. Opposite: Another-worldly landscape on Maui formed by (Haleakala volcano. crater.)

Kilauea (pictured here and opposite) *and Mauna Loa at Volcanoes National Park on the island of Hawaii, the most active volcanoes in the world, are a popular tourist attraction. The exquisite "ejecta," or the explosion of cinders and other matter during the eruption, proves that the goddess Pele is alive and well.* Overleaf: *Fiery lava being carried along by the surf from the peaks in Volcanoes National Park.*

Opposite: *Sculpted by the elements, lava has formed fierce-looking bluffs along the Puna coast.* This page: *The Devastation Trail in Volcanoes National Park, the result of an eruption in 1959 of Kilauea Iki (Little Kilauea) is a macabre forest of dead ohia trees in a carpet of pumice.ii Snow covers Mauna Loa and Mauna Kea from December until May (and sometimes July), to the delight of skiers.*

MOLOKAI

Known as "the friendly island," Molokai is a half-rainy, half-arid island, 38 miles long and about ten miles wide. Formed by three volcanoes, the island features breathtaking cliffs and jungle-like valleys with majestic Mount Kamakaou punctuating the eastern end. The major village, Kaunakakai, is actually a tiny enclave without so much as a traffic light. Nevertheless, everyone on the island congregates here, and Molokai has become an increasingly popular tourist center.

Molokai is best known as the sight of the Kalaupapa leper colony, located on the isolated Makanalua Peninsula, where an heroic Belgian priest, Father Damien, worked to aid those suffering from Hansen's disease.

MAUI

The slogan *Maui no ka oi* translates as "Maui is the best," and a growing number of residents and visitors seem to agree. The second largest island in the Hawaiian chain began as two separate land masses—the West Maui Mountains and the region of the powerful Haleakala. The fertile area that now joins them was created by erosion from the slopes of the two ranges, and today fields of sugar cane and pineapple blanket the plain.

Along the west coast, from the West Maui Mountains to Haleakala, sumptuous resorts and residential communities have cropped up near the beaches, while the quieter east coast reflects the charm of early island life. Haleakala Crater, the world's largest crater, and Puu Kukui—remnants of extinct volcanoes— are impressive natural sites.

KAUAI

Known as "The Garden Island" because of its lush vegetation, the result of over 400 inches of rainfall annually, Kauai is geologically the oldest island in the chain.

This page *and* opposite: *Lepers were banished to the Makanalua Peninsula of Molokai from 1866 until 1946. A Belgian priest, Father Damien, came to the island in 1873 to devote his life to their care. He contracted Hansen's disease and died in 1889. His body was returned to Belgium in 1936, but this gravestone marks the site of his first resting place. St. Philomena Church at Kalawao, Molokai, better known as Father Damien's Church, was completed in the late 1870s.*

Preceding page: *The Na Pali coast of northwestern Kauai.* This page *and* opposite: *The massive Na Pali cliffs rise 2,000 to 3,000 feet above sea level. Wind and rain have cut furrows into the ridges, making them verdant and beautiful. Its beaches are so isolated that only the most determined adventurer can find them, and only after a demanding two-mile-trek over the Kalalau trail.*

This page *and* opposite: *Other Kauai wonders. The sea pushes up through a shoreline lava tube at Horn Beach Park. According to legend, the moaning sound heard each time a geyser erupts is the cry of a long-trapped lizard in the tube. Waimea Canyon, "The Grand Canyon of the Pacific," offers an ever-changing palette of blues, reds, browns and greens.*

Preceding page: *The 2,875-foot deep, 10-mile long gorge was created eons ago by a crust fault.* This page: *Tobi Bridge, Kauai.* Opposite: *John Gregg Allerton created an exquisite garden on the site where Queen Emma, wife of King Kamehameha IV, had a garden a century ago. It is adjacent to the Pacific Tropical Botanical Garden, a 186-acre public paradise. Hanalei village on Kauai is the site of the 1837 Waioli Mission. The Wailoi Hui'ia Church, built in 1912, has a simple dignity that is most appealing. Kamokila, a reconstruction situated on a bend of the Wailua River, suggests what life must have been like in a Hawaiian village long ago.*

With the remote and exquisite Na Pali Coast along its northern edges, Mount Waialeale, its long-extinct volcano at its center, and the colorful Waimea Canyon, "The Grand Canyon of the Pacific," to the west, Kaui draws increasing numbers of tourists each year, eager to experience its great beauty.

NIIHAU, LANAI, AND KAHOOLAWE

For over a century, tiny Niihau, positioned just off the coast of Kauai, has been privately owned by the Robinson family. It can be visited only by special invitation. Its residents live simply, without electricity, automobiles, or television, and it is the only island where Hawaiian is the first language. English is taught in school, however.

In ancient times, Lanai was thought to be a cursed island where evil spirits lurked. Lanai lacks the ideal climate of the other islands— the east side being wet and gouged with uninhabitable gulches, while the rest of the island is dry and almost devoid of vegetation. Nevertheless, Lanai is perfect for growing pineapples. Thus, the Dole family bought almost the entire island in 1921, and eventually turned Lanai into one of the largest pineapple plantations in the world, which it remains to this day.

Maui offers a study in contrasts: developed areas like Kaanapali Beach on the west coast, and unspoiled Haleakala, with sugar cane fields (pictured here) and endless expanses of pastures. The Hana Highway (opposite) winds up the eastern coast of Maui toward a remote village, "Heavenly" Hana, its called, not only because of its great natural beauty but also because it suggests the tranquility of old Hawaii.

Kahoolawe, located off the west coast of Maui, is one of the most hotly contested parcels of land in the state. It is inhabited primarily by the U.S. military who use the island for target practice. Kahoolawe is a sacred island, however, the site of many ancient temples and shrines, and the Kahoolawe Ohana ("family") want the island to be properly preserved. A mini-war wages, but Kahoolawe has already been named a National Historic Site, and may soon be open to tourists.

THE ALOHA STATE

The word *aloha* in the Hawaiian language means many things, including "welcome," "farewell," and most especially, "love." Somehow that's especially fitting: a sobriquet with many meanings for a state with so many nationalities.

This page: *Haleakala Volcano last erupted in 1790 — "recently" in geological terms — and thus is said to be "dormant" rather than "extinct." Haleakala means "the house of the sun," and the sun does play mythic games with the landscape, making the craters blindingly beautiful at midday and evanescent at sunrise and sunset. Beauty of another sort is apparent in this unusual place: the rare silversword. The plant grows for 4 to 20 years before sending up a single 2- to 9-foot flower stalk. It blooms for one short season, then dies.* Opposite: *This giant Buddha at the Jodo Mission on Maui was dedicated in 1968 on the centennial of Japanese immigration.*

Hawaiian's honor the memory of Father Damien and his work among the lepers of Molokai with monuments such as this on Maui. Below: A ship like Carthaginian evokes Maui's whaling past. Opposite: An aerial view of Maui.

Index of Photography

All photographs courtesy of The Image Bank,
except those listed "Stockphotos, Inc."